WORLD OF MAMMALS

CHIMPANZEES

By Sophie Lockwood

Content Adviser: Barbara E. Brown, Scientific Associate, Mammal Division, Field Museum of Chicago

THE CHILD'S WORLD®, MANKATO, MINNESOTA

Chimpanzees

Published in the United States of America by The Child's World®
1980 Lookout Drive • Mankato, MN 56003-1705
800-599-READ • www.childsworld.com

Acknowledgements:

The Child's World®: Mary Berendes, Publishing Director

The Creative Spark: Mary Francis, Project Director; Wendy Mead, Editor; Deborah Goodsite, Photo Researcher

The Design Lab: Kathleen Petelinsek, Designer and Production Artist

Photos:

Cover: A & M SHAH/Animals Animals—Earth Scenes; Frontispiece and page 4: Ira Struebel/iStockphoto.com; half title: Kitch Bain/iStockphoto.com.

Interior: Animals Animals—Earth Scenes: 21 (Juergen & Christine Sohns), 24 (OSF/Michael Birkhead); Getty Images: 27 (Anup Shah); Jupiter Images: 9 (Michael Richards/Oxford Scientific), 5 top left and 12, 16 (Clive Bromhall/Oxford Scientific); Landov: 5 bottom right and 30 (Finbarr O'Reilly/Reuters); Minden Pictures: 11 (Anup Shah/npl), 15 (Ingo Arndt), 29 (Frans Lanting); Panos Pictures: 33 (Sven Torfinn), 5 bottom left and 36 (Penny Tweedie); Photolibrary Group: 5 top right and 18, 5 center left and 23; Photo Researchers, Inc.: 35 (Georg Gerster).

Library of Congress Cataloging-in-Publication Data

Lockwood, Sophie.
 Chimpanzees / by Sophie Lockwood.
   p. cm. — (The world of mammals)
 Includes index.
 ISBN 978-1-59296-927-2 (library bound : alk. paper)
 1. Chimpanzees—Juvenile literature. I. Title. II. Series.
 QL737.P96L63 2008
 599.885—dc22   2007020870

TABLE OF CONTENTS

Chapter One

Mother and Child

This is the story of Gira and her son, Gando. Immediately after giving birth, Gira helps her baby nurse at her breast. She cradles Gando in her arms, touching his face and caressing his body. Although this scene could take place in any hospital, it is actually taking place in the forests of Taï National Park in the Ivory Coast, Africa. This tender, caring mother is not human, but close to it. Gira is a chimpanzee.

As chimpanzees go, Gando is large for an infant. He weighs 2 kilograms (4.4 pounds). For the first few days, Gira clings tightly to Gando, who is as helpless as a human newborn. By **instinct,** he begins clutching her fur. Even so, she keeps a protective arm around him—his grip can only hold him for a short time. For his first month, mother and child live chest-to-chest. Gira never puts Gando down or leaves him. For a chimpanzee, motherhood is twenty-four hours a day, seven days a week. For the first three to four years of Gando's life, Gira will never be more than about 5 meters (16.4 feet) away.

This map shows the habitat range for common chimpanzees and bonobos, a related species.

At two months old, Gando can finally support himself well enough to hold his own weight. While Gira forages for food, he holds tight, drinking milk from her nipple whenever he gets hungry. She will allow him to nurse until he is about three to four years old. At three to six months old, Gando stays close, traveling chest-to-chest with his mother. From six months to six years old, the youngster will be carried on his mother's back.

Each night, Gira quickly builds a sleeping nest in a tree. Gando tucks in next to her and is lulled to sleep as she grooms his fur. The bond between a mother chimpanzee and her son is strong and will last a lifetime.

Gira is twenty-nine, and Gando is her fourth child. She has the experience to successfully raise a baby. Chimpanzee offspring mature very slowly compared to most other wild species. A newborn wildebeest can stand and run on the day it is born. Two-month-old giraffes nibble on acacia leaves. Lion cubs can usually hunt for themselves by age two or three.

Gando will be considered a baby until he is six. He spends most of his time with Gira but also plays with other babies, under Gira's watchful eye. He is very lively and loves to be tickled.

From six to nine years old, Gando is a juvenile. He and other males his age chase each other through shrubs, climb

A young chimpanzee enjoys a snack in the Taï National Park.

Did You Know?
Scientists refer to male chimps between twelve and fifteen years old and female chimps between ten and thirteen years old as subadults.

trees, and swing from the limbs. This period is followed by adolescence, and then adulthood, at about fifteen years old. With luck, Gando may live to be forty years old in the wild. The lessons he learns as a child last a long time.

USING TOOLS

One of the biggest challenges a chimpanzee faces is foraging for food. What is good to eat? What is not? How do I get that food? Chimps eat like humans—they are **omnivores.** Nearly half of the chimps' diet is fruit, but they also eat leaves, leaf buds, nuts, seeds, flowers, bark, stems, and resin. They round out this vegetarian diet by eating insects, birds, birds' eggs, and small- or medium-size mammals, mainly antelopes, baboons, and other monkeys, especially the colobus monkey.

In the forest, nuts are plentiful. Eating nuts, however, takes some skill, since most nuts have hard shells. By the time Gando is five years old, Gira has taught him how to crack nutshells using a hammer and anvil. The hammer is a large rock. The anvil is any flat rock or tree root.

Cracking nutshells takes practice. Gando chooses a stone to use as a hammer, but he has no luck breaking the shells.

Gira allows him to struggle for a few minutes. When she is sure he cannot succeed, she goes over and takes the stone. Slowly,

Chimpanzees like this one learn how to get food by using tools.

she turns the stone around, finds just the right position, and cracks a nut. She cracks several nuts, showing Gando what to do and letting him enjoy the nutmeat. Gando watches carefully. When it is again his turn, he adjusts the stone to the exact same position Gira

A chimpanzee uses a rock to break open some palm nuts.

used and successfully cracks a nut. Gira has taught her son a valuable lesson.

During his life, Gira will also teach him how to fish for termites in a nest. She'll choose a stick of the right length and thickness, strip off the leaves, and carefully dip the stick into a hole in the termite nest. Gando must practice termite fishing many times before he can pull a stick out with the termites still attached.

Gando also learns how to use leaves like sponges to sop up drinking water. He learns which fruits are edible and when they are ripe. He will learn to eat clay if his stomach is upset and to use certain leaves to help heal wounds.

Gando will also groom his friends and relatives. Grooming is a key activity in chimpanzee life. It gets rid of dirt, lice, dead skin, and bugs in chimp fur. It also builds strong ties between two chimps. Chimps form real friendships, and good friends groom each other. It is part of being a member of a chimpanzee community.

Would You Believe?
Some chimpanzees have a sweet tooth. They use long, thin sticks to scoop honey from wild beehives without getting stung! Chimps know the difference between stinging and stingless bees, and use shorter sticks when getting sweet treats from the stingless variety.

Did You Know?
Adult male chimps groom each other more than the females do.

Chapter Two

Community Life

As dawn breaks over Gombe National Park in Tanzania, the local residents climb down from their night nests to begin the day's work. Chimpanzees spend most of their days finding and eating food. They are most active in the early morning, late afternoon, and early evening, spending six to eight hours a day feeding.

Friends or relatives forage together in small groups. Suddenly, a whoop of "pant-hoots" echoes throughout the forest. Foraging chimps raise their heads and listen. They rush to where the calls come from. It is a great find—a huge fig tree, heavy with ripe fruit. Chimps love figs, and sharing such a find is common among troop members.

Chimpanzee communities are "**fission-fusion**" groups. Fission-fusion sounds complicated, but it is really simple. It just means that members come and go as they please. They separate (fission) to sleep, forage, and eat. They come together (fusion) to protect their territory.

Within the community, every chimpanzee has a social position. The higher the rank, the greater the privileges

the chimp enjoys. One **dominant** male, called the **alpha male,** rules the chimpanzee troop.

RULING THE ROOST

Rico has been the alpha male of a troop for several years and has fathered many of the males in his troop. Now he is past his prime. Savu, a young adult of twenty-five, has decided to challenge him for the job of alpha male. He is handsome, ambitious, and strong.

An alpha male walks around in Gombe National Park.

Did You Know?
A chimpanzee usually builds a new sleeping nest every night. Pick a fork in a tree. Reinforce it with branches. Pad it with leaves. An experienced nest builder can create a comfortable sleeping nest in about one minute.

Head to toe, he measures 1.6 meters (5.3 feet)—at the high end of male chimpanzee height. He clearly has eaten well, weighing in at just over 60 kilograms (132 pounds).

Taking over as alpha male is not quick or easy. Savu must challenge and defeat several other males on his way up the social ladder. Luckily, he has two strong brothers who stand by him. It may take weeks or months for Savu to reach a high enough status to challenge Rico directly. When he does, the challenge is brutal. Rico also has loyal friends who support him.

While males may fight for dominance, female chimps, such as this mother with her baby, can also be aggressive.

Would You Believe?
Chimpanzees may be shorter and weigh less than adult humans, but they are five to six times stronger. Do not arm wrestle with a chimp— you'll lose!

Savu is not successful on the first try, but succeeds after several challenges. His brothers now rise in status within the troop. Top male rank means first access to food and mating rights with females. As alpha male, Savu must keep the peace within the troop and protect his community from attack by other chimp troops. Other high-ranking males, like Savu's brothers, also enjoy mating rights with females. It is one reason to support the alpha male.

Now that Savu is the troop's alpha male, the females will become interested in mating with him. They want to mate with strong males. The **genetic** makeup of a strong mate helps produce strong, healthy children. Females can be up to 30 centimeters (1 foot) shorter than males and can weigh more than 26 kilograms (57 pounds) less. Smart females know that having a powerful male in charge adds to the troop's safety.

Females can breed throughout the year and can mate about every thirty-six days. When they are ready for mating, their **genital** area on the rump swells noticeably. This fertile period is called **estrus.** Interested males recognize this sign and announce their interest in mating. Females choose mates carefully and may mate several times with several different males.

Females are pregnant for about eight months. They deliver single babies—twins are rare. Once a baby is born, a female dedicates herself to raising and protecting that child.

Females can begin having offspring at thirteen or fourteen years old. At that time, females shop around for new troops to join. Among chimpanzees, the females leave their birth troops, and the males stay. Males welcome new females into their community. It gives the males opportunities to father offspring and increase their troop's population.

A female can have a new child every four to five years. Some female chimpanzees delay having more children to concentrate efforts on their current children. The males may be bigger, but the females can choose their own mates and determine when they will mate.

Female chimps form a close bond with their children.

Chapter Three

So Nearly Human

Chimpanzees belong to a group of **primates** called the great apes. That category includes gorillas, chimpanzees, bonobos, and orangutans. One additional species is included with in the category of great apes—humans.

Common chimpanzees and humans are related. We both laugh at jokes. We feel fear, sadness, loss, and love. We hug, kiss, and touch each other with affection. We communicate those emotions through sound, body language, and facial expressions. The main differences are that humans have better developed speech patterns, and we like to think we are smarter. Chimps are exceptionally intelligent. When they are faced with problems, they can reason out solutions. They make and use tools and often play jokes on their friends.

While monkeys are exceptionally noisy, great apes only speak when they have something to say. Chimpanzee speech includes thirteen different types of calls. They make shrill screams, grunts, moans,

Would You Believe?
Chimpanzees share 98.4 percent of our DNA, the genetic material of an animal or plant. In fact, chimpanzees and bonobos are closer to humans than they are to gorillas or to any other primates. And recent research shows that humans are even more closely related to bonobos than to common chimpanzees.

whimpers, and "pant-hoots." They cannot create speech in the same way as humans because their vocal cords are not built the same way. However, chimps have no problems letting others know what they are thinking or feeling. They combine sounds with body gestures or facial expressions to communicate, which shows their intelligence.

Haji hears a cry in the forest. She immediately recognizes the voice as belonging to Weezie, a close friend. Weezie is clearly upset. Haji hurries to her friend's side. When Haji arrives, she sees that Weezie's two-year-old daughter has been injured.

Chimps have distinctive voices. Some are higher or lower pitched. Other voices are louder or quieter. Troop members can recognize the voices of other troop members. This is the same identification skill that humans use when a friend calls on the telephone.

Chimpanzee Calls

CALL	EMOTION
Wraa	Fear
Huu	Puzzlement
Soft barking or coughing sound	Annoyance
Aaa—related to food	Enjoyment
Crying	Rage or distress
Arrival pant-hoot	Excitement

Source: Jane Goodall Institute

Hand gestures are also important when chimps communicate. Abie is across a clearing from his brother Cam. He stands up and scratches his body in a specific place. Cam immediately stands and scratches in the exact same place. Within a few minutes, Cam comes over to groom Abie.

Body language is an important way of saying, "I submit to you." Crouching down, presenting the rump, or holding out a hand are means of showing **submission.** Chimps have a social order, with alpha chimps in charge

Chimpanzees communicate with sounds, facial expressions, and gestures.

and lower-ranked chimps below them. Higher rank comes with privileges and responsibility. The alpha male of a troop defends the troop against attacks by other chimps and must recognize possible danger. Lower-ranked chimps show submission to the alpha male to acknowledge that the alpha is the boss. If they do not, they may be forced out of the troop and lose protection, family ties, and friendships.

As for facial gestures, toothy grins usually mean fear. A grimace or frown shows aggression. Wide-open eyes and mouth indicate excitement, while lips squeezed together are usually seen during fights. A pout probably shows interest in something, particularly food. When a male chimp sees a female he likes, he flips his lip for her.

CHIMPS ON PATROL

Savu organizes a patrol through a part of the troop's territory. This area has not been visited recently, and Savu wants to make sure no competing troops are invading his turf. The chimp patrol moves silently through the brush in single file. They are nervous, quickly upset, and alert.

A bird takes flight, rustling the bushes directly ahead. The chimps react with fear, touching each other for comfort and

Did You Know?
Chimpanzees and bonobos can be trained to communicate with humans using American Sign Language and keyboards with symbols. Kanzi, a bonobo working with scientist Sue Savage-Rumbaugh, has sentence-building and comprehension skills equal to those of a child at 32 months of age.

showing fear grins. Farther along the path, the chimps find the body of a dead monkey. Although chimps hunt and eat monkeys, they examine the body and pass on by. Chimps never eat **carrion.**

Savu sees two juvenile chimps and a single adult female foraging in a thicket. The chimp patrol approaches warily. Then Savu's troop explodes. They attack the foreigners, screaming, waving their arms, and stamping their feet. They also shake broken branches in a threatening way. The outsiders run for their lives. Chimps that find outsiders in their territories will attack and kill or maim the invaders. They only avoid a fight if there are two or more large males in the offending group. Those males could be dangerous.

A smile can be a sign of fear, not happiness, for a chimpanzee.

THE HUNT

Although chimpanzees do not eat meat often, when they do, they prefer colobus monkey. In Gombe, chimps hunt red colobus monkeys, wild pigs, and small antelopes. Gombe chimps hunt alone, catching about 150 animals yearly. They prey on infant and juvenile monkeys or prey that is obviously weak.

Chimpanzees can work together to hunt for food.

For chimps in Taï National Park, hunting is a group event. It takes about six male chimps to catch one monkey. Each chimp has a specific job. One chimp is a driver. This ape must make sure that several monkeys head in the direction of the other chimp hunters. By getting behind the monkeys and making threatening noises, the driver herds the monkeys toward the ambusher. As the monkeys flee, chimps take up positions on either side, forming a chute through which the monkeys must pass. Chaser chimps help the driver keep the monkeys moving in the right direction—straight toward the ambusher. Blocker chimps prevent the monkeys from escaping by making noise and threatening gestures on both sides of the fleeing monkeys. The ambusher, an experienced hunter, waits for his prey to arrive. If five monkeys head in the ambusher's direction, the ambusher will probably catch dinner for the day. The kill is quick, and all the hunters share the meat. This hunting technique is similar to that probably employed by early human hunter-gatherer clans.

Hunting is social in some regards and selfish in others. Some hunters work together. Others work alone. The most human aspect of chimp hunting is the willingness of the hunter to share his catch with others.

Chapter Four

Types of Chimpanzees

Chimpanzees fall into two scientific groups: *Pan troglodytes* (common chimpanzees) and *Pan paniscus* (bonobos or pygmy chimpanzees). For many years, scientists believed that bonobos were simply small chimpanzees. Recently, however, scientists have determined that bonobos are a distinct species, closely related to chimpanzees.

All common chimpanzees have coarse brown or black hair. The young have a white tuft on their rumps, which disappears as they get older. They have flat noses and large ears that stick out. The face, fingers, toes, palms of the hands, and soles of the feet are bare skin. As they age, chimps may go gray, just like elderly humans. Females average 26 to 50 kilograms (57.3 to 110.2 pounds), and males are larger—50 to 70 kilograms (110.2 to 154.3 pounds). Body length is usually 1 to 1.7 meters (3.3 to 5.6 feet) from head to toe.

Chimpanzees are **quadrupeds,** which mean they walk on all fours. Their arms tend to be longer than their legs, so when they walk, their backs are lower than their heads

and shoulders. This allows them to look forward instead of down. They protect their hands by bearing their weight on their knuckles. Chimps can walk on two feet over short distances, but knuckle-walking is easier and faster.

Chimpanzee hands have the same basic shape as human hands. They have flexible fingers and opposable thumbs. This means that they can use their hands for grasping objects. Chimp thumbs are shorter, and a chimp cannot touch the tips of the thumb and forefinger together. All fingers (and toes) have nails rather than claws. Chimp feet look much like human feet, but the big toe is longer, more flexible, and more useful than human big toes. A chimp foot can grab and hold items, which a human foot cannot do well.

Chimpanzees use their hands much like humans do.

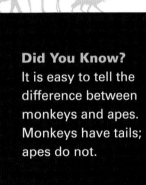

Did You Know?
It is easy to tell the difference between monkeys and apes. Monkeys have tails; apes do not.

Western, central, and eastern chimpanzees are the three main subspecies of common chimpanzees. Fewer than 56,000 western chimpanzees remain in wild portions of Ghana, Guinea, Ivory Coast, Liberia, Senegal, Sierra Leone, and Togo. These chimps prefer to live along rivers in forests and in rain forests, up to 2,000 meters (6,562 feet) above sea level.

Central common chimpanzees can be found in the rain forests and open woodlands of Cameroon, Central African Republic, Congo, Gabon, Nigeria, and Zaire. Scientists believe that there are about 70,000 to 115,000 central chimpanzees left. Eastern common chimpanzees live in Burundi, Central African Republic, Rwanda, Sudan, Tanzania, Uganda, and Zaire. They enjoy a variety of habitats, from dry savanna to rain forests, up to 2,000 meters (6,562 feet) above sea level. The current population estimate for eastern chimpanzees is 76,000 to 120,000 apes.

BONOBOS

Differences between chimps and bonobos are few. Bonobos have longer legs, shorter arms, and a narrower torso. They tend to be smaller than common chimpanzees, hence the nickname pygmy chimpanzee. Bonobos have mostly black

skin and a central parting of the hair on their heads. They have smaller ears and walk more upright than common chimpanzees. Bonobos are more humanlike and more peaceful than common chimpanzees. They are found mostly in the Democratic Republic of Congo. Population estimates for bonobos range from 5,000 to 50,000, although the smaller number is likely to be more accurate. Bonobos are more endangered than common chimpanzees.

Social relationships are extremely important to bonobos. They belong to large communities of up to eighty individuals. Subgroups of two to fifteen bonobos that

Bonobos live together in large groups.

forage together are usually related through the mother. When two bonobos meet, they hug, kiss, and fondle each other.

Bonobos are the smallest of the great apes. Male bonobos are larger than the females. On average, males weigh around 39 kilograms (86 pounds) and females weigh about 31 kilograms (68 pounds). Both males and females can range in height from 70 to 119 centimeters (27.6 to 47 inches). Although they are called pygmy chimps, the largest bonobos are about the same size as smaller common chimpanzees.

Did You Know?
When a group of bonobos travels along the ground, they bend branches to mark the trail for others to follow.

Bonobos form strong relationships with each other.

Chapter Five

The Past, Present, and Future

In a cornfield in western Uganda, a young woman and her toddler come face to face with a male chimpanzee. The woman screams and runs away as fast as she can. In her village, chimpanzees have attacked young children fifteen times in seven years.

The chimps are hungry, and both the village and cornfield lie in their natural territory. Toddlers, about the size of colobus monkeys, appear to be game to chimps. One chimp named Saddam has become increasingly bold during the last few years. He has even snatched children from inside their homes.

Whatever the reason behind the attacks, local chimps have become more violent. Villagers regularly find the

Did You Know?
In 2002, the World Wildlife Fund began the African Great Apes Program to save core populations of all ape species in Africa. This program is designed to save gorillas, bonobos, and chimpanzees and their habitats.

remnants of chimp meals strewn in their fields—banana peels, broken stalks of sugarcane, and half-eaten ears of corn.

This situation represents an ongoing problem that chimpanzee communities face—loss of habitat. Habitat loss, combined with human diseases, **poaching,** and bush-meat trading, put chimpanzees in danger of **extinction.**

How did human's closest relative reach endangered status? Africa's human population has increased by 400 percent in the past one hundred years. The population continues to grow at a rate of 3 percent each year. People need homes, food, and transportation. Rain forests where chimpanzees normally make their homes have been cleared to make way for villages and farmland.

Logging companies plow roads through chimpanzee habitats, cut down trees, and destroy the ecosystem. The human need for lumber is continual. Thus, chimpanzee habitats become smaller and farther apart. Human actions have turned one large rain forest into several small clusters of forest. The battle for space is on—and the chimps are losing.

Closer contact with humans has brought human diseases to the great apes. Chimpanzees easily catch common colds, pneumonia, HIV, polio, and Ebola. There is no way to give medicine to sick chimpanzees. Pneumonia, easily cured in humans, often leads to death for chimpanzees.

When chimps have **contagious** diseases, they spread that illness to other members of their troops.

In 2005, the deadly Ebola virus spread among gorillas and chimpanzees. Ebola destroys the body's internal

The cutting down of trees in the rain forests is destroying chimpanzee habitats.

organs, and victims bleed to death. In Odzala National Park in the Congo basin, rangers had to stand by helplessly as thousands of chimpanzees died from Ebola. Hopefully, a vaccine will stop the outbreaks. However, no vaccine can replace thousands of individual animals. Chimpanzees breed so slowly that restoring the population will take many years.

Even in areas where chimpanzees are protected by law, poaching takes far too many chimpanzees. Poachers trap chimps for two reasons—wildlife and bushmeat trading. Many people think that having a pet chimp would be great fun. However, baby chimps grow up to be adult chimps, and the adults get aggressive and are difficult to control. They can never be housebroken and have to wear diapers. Chimps and bonobos have also been sold to medical research labs to use for experiments. These animals have been used to study diseases and to test medicines.

For centuries, Africans have eaten bushmeat—the meat of wild animals—as their main source of protein. As more Africans move into cities, the market for bushmeat has moved with them. In the Congo, poachers kill chimps for bushmeat at a rate that is 5 to 7 percent faster than the chimps normally reproduce.

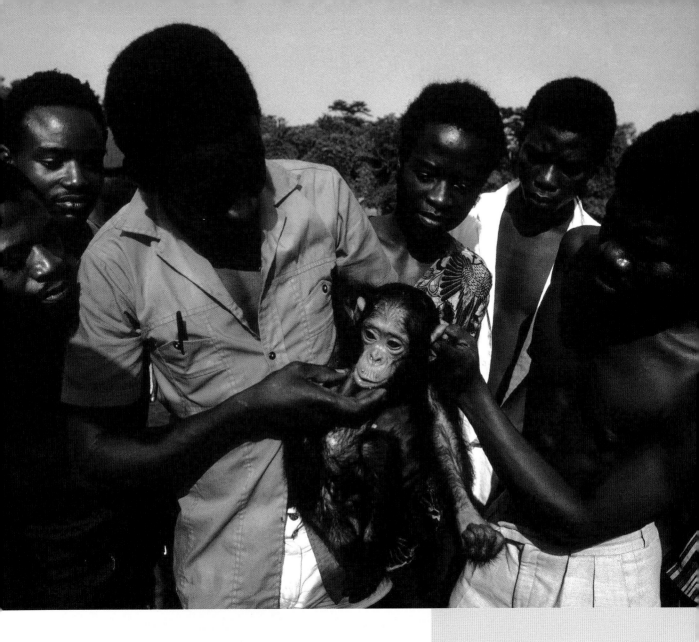

SOLUTIONS

Zoos and conservation centers from around the world developed a Species Survival Plan for chimpanzees in 1989.

A poacher tries to sell a young chimpanzee.

Did You Know?
Chimpanzees live in forty accredited zoos in the United States. The American Association of Zoos and Aquariums promotes better facilities and compounds for chimps, including climbing frames and mental games.

The program calls for recording mating events and the offspring production of chimps in zoos and sanctuaries. Participating zoos support research into chimpanzee care and behavior. Public education about chimpanzee problems is part of the survival plan.

Wildlife conservation groups work with government officials to establish preserves and sanctuaries. Groups purchase land for preserves. They help train and equip park rangers to reduce poaching. These groups also provide educational programs for schools and parks to increase public understanding of the problems.

Chimpanzees are considered a **flagship species,** which is a species that attracts public interest and funding. When a conservation group supports a flagship species, all other species living in the same area or that are dependent on the flagship species will thrive. Efforts to save chimpanzees from extinction will save other animals in their region. It is easy to raise money to help save such popular species. While money helps, humans must be aware that they have created the problems facing chimpanzees today. It is our responsibility to save our closest relatives—and, perhaps, ourselves as well.

A veterinarian examines a chimpanzee living in a sanctuary in Uganda.

Glossary

alpha male (AL-fuh MAYL) most powerful or dominant animal in a group; group leader

carrion (KAYR-ee-un) dead and rotting flesh

contagious (kun-TAY-juss) able to be transmitted from one animal to another, usually by touching or through the air

dominant (DAHM-ih-nunt) in control or command of others

estrus (ESS-truss) period during which a female animal is most receptive to mating

extinction (eks-TINK-shun) the state of a plant or animal no longer existing

fission-fusion (FISH-un FYOO-zhun) a social structure in which animals in a group have periods when they work, sleep, feed, or play separately (fission) and then come together for other activities (fusion)

flagship species (FLAG-ship SPEE-sheez) endangered or threatened animal species that attract a great deal of public interest and funding, such as whales or giant pandas

genital (JEN-ih-tul) referring to an animal's reproductive organs

genetic (juh-NEH-tik) studying the chemical substances that make up animal or plant characteristics

instinct (IN-stinkt) one's natural sense of how to act

omnivores (OM-nuh-vawrz) animals that eat both animals and plants

poaching (POH-ching) hunting animals without permission

primates (PRY-maytz) members of an order of mammals with a large brain and complex hands and feet, such as humans, monkeys, and apes

quadrupeds (KWAHD-ruh-pedz) animals with four feet

submission (sub-MIS-shun) the act of showing that another creature is more powerful

For More Information

Watch It

Jane Goodall's Return to Gombe, DVD (Culver City, CA: Sony Pictures, 2005)

Jane Goodall's Wild Chimpanzees, DVD (Burbank, CA: Sling Shot, 2003)

Nature: Chimpanzees, DVD (Chicago: Questar, 2003)

Read It

Bow, Patricia. *Chimpanzee Rescue: Changing the Future for Endangered Wildlife.* Richmond Hill, Ontario: Firefly Books, 2004.

Constable, Tamsin. *Chimpanzees: Social Climbers of the Forest.* New York: Dorling Kindersley, 2000.

Donovan, Sandra. *Chimpanzees.* Chicago: Raintree, 2002.

Goodall, Jane. *Chimpanzees I Love: Saving their World and Ours.* New York: Scholastic Press, 2001.

Spilsbury, Richard. *Chimpanzees—Life in a Troop.* Chicago: Heinemann Educational Books, 2003.

Look It Up

Visit our Web page for lots of links about chimpanzees:
http://www.childsworld.com/links

Note to Parents, Teachers, and Librarians: We routinely verify our Web links to make sure they are safe, active sites—so encourage your readers to check them out!

The Animal Kingdom
Where Do Chimpanzees Fit In?

Kingdom: Animalia

Phylum: Chordatata (animals with backbones)

Class: Mammalia

Order: Primates

Family: Hominidae

Genus: *Pan*

Species: *Pan troglodytes*
Pan paniscus

Index

About the Author

Sophie Lockwood is a former teacher and a longtime writer. She writes textbooks, newspaper articles, and magazine articles. Sophie enjoys writing about animals and their habits. The most interesting part of her research, Sophie says, is learning how scientists apply their knowledge to save endangered species. She lives with her husband in the foothills of the Blue Ridge Mountains.